Tiger Shark Files

by E. C. Andrews

Minneapolis, Minnesota

Credits
Images are courtesy of Shutterstock.com. With thanks to Getty Images, Thinkstock Photo, and iStockphoto. Recurring – schab, nabil refaat, Maquiladora, A.Aruno. Cover – hvostik, Martin Voeller. 4–5 – Derek Heasley, EDGAR PHOTOSAPIENS. 6–7 – Martin Voeller, Vladislav Klimin. 8–9 – frantisekhojdysz, Martin Voeller. 10–11 – Joe Dordo Brnobic, frantisekhojdysz. 12–13 – Martin Prochazkacz, Ethan Daniels. 14–15 – Tomas Kotouc, Alex Rush, Matt9122. 16–17 – WorldTHROUGHme, Kristina Vackova. 18–19 – Paul Winkworth, FtLaudGirl. 20–21 – Steve Hinczynski, Tomas Kotouc. 22–23 – Natalya Chernyavskaya, Tomas Kotouc.

Bearport Publishing Company Product Development Team
President: Jen Jenson; Director of Product Development: Spencer Brinker; Managing Editor: Allison Juda; Associate Editor: Naomi Reich; Associate Editor: Tiana Tran; Art Director: Colin O'Dea; Designer: Kim Jones; Designer: Kayla Eggert; Product Development Assistant: Owen Hamlin

Library of Congress Cataloging-in-Publication Data is available at www.loc.gov or upon request from the publisher.

ISBN: 979-8-89232-063-4 (hardcover)
ISBN: 979-8-89232-537-0 (paperback)
ISBN: 979-8-89232-196-9 (ebook)

© 2025 BookLife Publishing
This edition is published by arrangement with BookLife Publishing.

North American adaptations © 2025 Bearport Publishing Company. All rights reserved. No part of this publication may be reproduced in whole or in part, stored in any retrieval system, or transmitted in any form or by any means, electronic, mechanical, photocopying, recording, or otherwise, without written permission from the publisher. Bearport Publishing is a division of Chrysalis Education Group.

For more information, write to Bearport Publishing, 5357 Penn Avenue South, Minneapolis, MN 55419.

CONTENTS

The Tiger Shark..............4
Diet........................6
Mouth 8
Nose.......................10
Eyes 12
Skin.......................14
Skeleton 16
Fins.......................18
Tail 20
Life Cycle 22
Glossary 24
Index......................24

THE TIGER SHARK

There are more than 500 kinds of sharks. Tiger sharks are some of the deadliest.

Tiger sharks are the fourth largest kind of shark. They normally live by themselves.

DIET

Tiger sharks are powerful **predators**. They eat just about anything they can find.

These sharks hunt other fish, turtles, birds, and more. Tiger sharks have even been known to eat trash!

MOUTH

There are about 48 teeth in a tiger shark's mouth. Each sharp tooth is curved and has **serrated** edges.

A tiger shark uses its strong teeth to hold on to its **prey**. Then, the predator shakes its head back and forth. This rips its meal into small pieces.

NOSE

Tiger sharks have a strong sense of smell. This helps them sniff out their prey.

The flat shape of their noses allows them to turn very quickly. It also helps the sharks trap prey against rocks.

EYES

Tiger sharks can see very well in dark water. This is helpful since they hunt mostly at night.

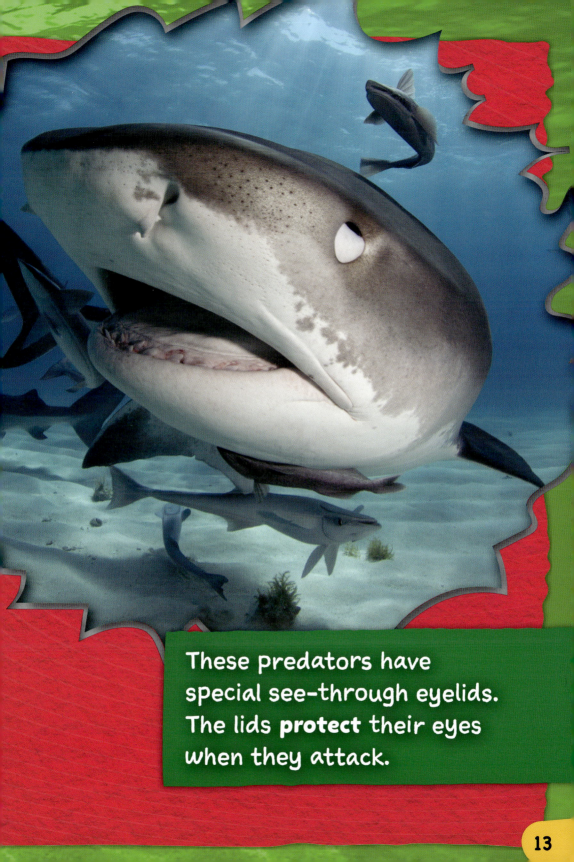

These predators have special see-through eyelids. The lids **protect** their eyes when they attack.

SKIN

Tiger sharks are covered in many tiny, pointed **scales**. Together, the scales make their skin very tough.

The sharks get their name from the stripes on their skin. These stripes look similar to those of a tiger.

SKELETON

Sharks do not have bones. Their skeletons are made of **cartilage**. Cartilage is softer and more bendy than bone.

Cartilage is lighter than bone, too. This makes it easier for tiger sharks to swim and float.

FINS

Tiger sharks have a few different kinds of fins. Each helps them do different things.

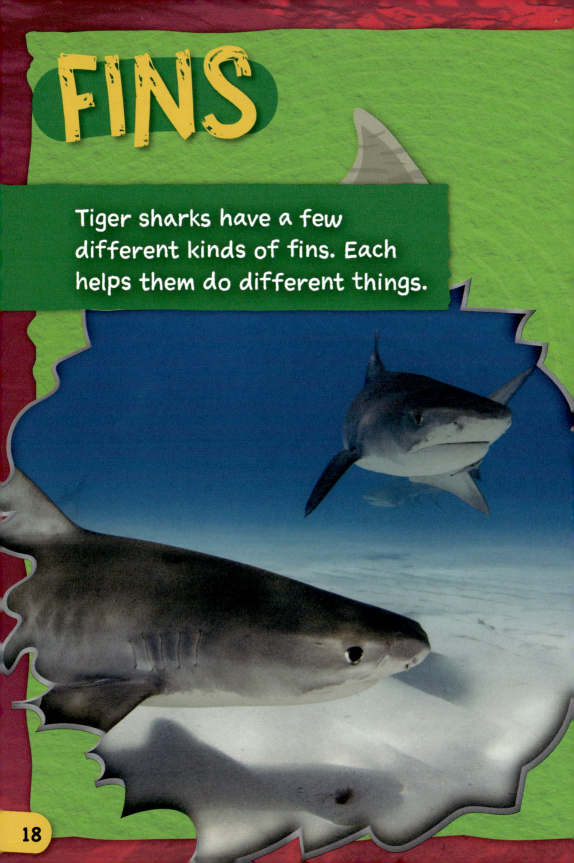

The dorsal fin on a tiger shark's back keeps it from rolling over. Pectoral (PEK-tur-uhl) fins stick out from its sides. These help the shark turn.

TAIL

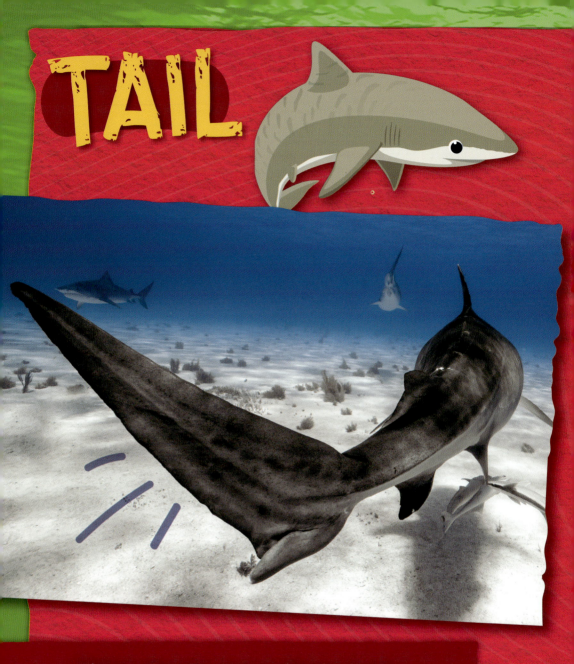

Tiger sharks move their tails from side to side when swimming. This pushes them forward.

Most of the time, tiger sharks are slow swimmers. However, they can move very quickly while hunting.

LIFE CYCLE

Baby tiger sharks are called pups. They **hatch** from eggs inside their mother's body.

The pups are on their own as soon as they are born. Tiger sharks can live for about 50 years.

GLOSSARY

cartilage the strong, rubbery stuff that makes up a shark's skeleton

hatch to come out of an egg

predators animals that hunt and eat other animals

prey an animal that is hunted and eaten by another animal

protect to keep something safe from harm

scales small, hard pieces that form a shark's skin

serrated having sharp, bumpy points

INDEX

cartilage 16–17
eyelids 13
fins 18–19
nose 10–11
prey 9–11
pups 22–23
scales 14
stripes 15
teeth 8–9